LATINOS IN BASEBALL

Pedro Martinez

Jim Gallagher

Mitchell Lane Publishers, Inc.
P.O. Box 200
Childs, MD 21916-0200

LATINOS IN BASEBALL

Tino Martinez	Bobby Bonilla	Roberto Alomar	**Pedro Martinez**
Moises Alou	Sammy Sosa	Ivan Rodriguez	Carlos Baerga
Ramon Martinez	Alex Rodriguez	Vinny Castilla	Mariano Rivera

Library of Congress Cataloging-in-Publication Data

Gallagher, Jim, 1969-
    Pedro Martinez / Jim Gallagher.
        p. cm. — (Latinos in baseball)
   Includes index.
   Summary: Presents a biography of the professional baseball pitcher from the Dominican Republic who won the National League's Cy Young Award in 1997.
   ISBN 1-883845-85-8 (lib. bdg.)
   1. Martinez, Pedro, 1971- —Juvenile literature. 2. Baseball players—Dominican Republic—Biography—Juvenile literature. [1. Martinez, Pedro, 1971- . 2. Baseball players. 3. Latin Americans—Biography.] I. Title. II. Series.
GV865. M355G35 1999
796.357' 092—dc2l
[B]
                                                98-48047
                                                  CIP
                                                    AC

About the Author: Jim Gallagher is a former newspaper editor and publisher. A graduate of LaSalle University, he lives near Philadelphia with his two dogs. His books include *The Composite Guide to Wrestling* (Chelsea House) and *Searching for Buried Treasure* (Chelsea House).

Photo Credits: cover: ©1998 Boston Red Sox; p. 4 ©1998 Boston Red Sox; p. 9 Reuters/Shaun Best/Archive Photos; pp. 11, 19 Fernando Cuza/Pedro Martinez; p. 22 UPI/Corbis-Bettmann; p. 26 J.D. Cuban/Allsport; p. 29 ©1998 Houston Astros; p. 33 Otto Greule/Allsport; pp. 35, 36, 38 Fernando Cuza/Pedro Martinez; p. 47 Reuters/Brian Snyder/Archive Photos; p. 49 AP Photo; pp. 53, 55 ©1998 Boston Red Sox; p. 61 Reuters/Jim Bourg/Archive Photos

Acknowledgments: This story has been thoroughly researched and checked for accuracy. To the best of our knowledge, it represents a true story.

Dedication: In memory of my dad, Don Gallagher, and all our backyard catches.

TABLE OF CONTENTS

CHAPTER ONE
Winning the Cy Young Award

Competition among National League pitchers for the 1997 Cy Young Award was intense. The prestigious prize, named after baseball's all-time winningest pitcher, is given each season to the best pitcher in the National and American leagues, as determined by a vote of sportswriters who cover baseball. When the '97 regular season ended in the last week of September, several National League pitchers had recorded excellent statistics. The especially strong field included Atlanta pitcher Greg Maddux, a four-time Cy Young Award–winner who had won 19 games and was second in the league with a 2.21 earned run average (ERA); his teammate Denny Neagle, who led the National League in victories with 20; Philadelphia's Curt Schilling, a 17-game winner and the league's strikeout leader with 319, a NL record for a right-handed pitcher; and Houston ace Darryl Kile, who had gone 19-7 with a 2.57 ERA. The number of pitchers who had particularly good seasons led *Sports Illustrated* to note in a late September article, "Whichever pitcher the Baseball Writers Association of America (BWAA) chooses, the vote is likely to be the closest in the National League since 1987. That year Philadelphia's Steve Bedrosian beat out Chicago's Rick Sutcliffe by just two votes and San Francisco's Rick Reuschel by three."

As it turned out, *Sports Illustrated* was mistaken. When the BWAA's votes were tallied in the second week of November 1997, one pitcher was far ahead of the rest of the field: Montreal Expos' ace Pedro Martinez, who received 134 votes to 75 by runner-up Maddux. They were followed by Neagle (24), Schilling (12), and Kile (7).

It was an excellent selection, as Martinez had been practically unhittable all season. Opposing batters managed just a .184 batting average against him during 1997, and he led the league with a phenomenal 1.90 ERA and 13 complete games. The 26-year-old fireballer became just the 14th pitcher in major-league history to strike out over 300 batters in a season, finishing with an NL second-best 305. He finished the year with a solid 17-8 record that appeared even more impressive considering that the Expos finished at just 78-84 and ranked 10th among the National League's 14 teams in runs scored.

Martinez, at his home in the Dominican Republic, was thrilled when he heard that he had won the award, but he remained humble, telling reporters, "I don't consider myself better than Maddux right now." He and his family then celebrated his becoming the first resident of the tiny and impoverished Caribbean nation to win the award, as well as the fourth Hispanic pitcher overall, joining Mike Cuellar (1969), Fernando Valenzuela (1981), and Willie Hernandez (1984).

When a ceremony was planned in Boston to honor Martinez as the NL's Cy Young Award–winner, one of his countrymen was asked to present the coveted trophy. The presenter, Juan Marichal, had several things in common with Pedro Martinez. Both had grown up in the Dominican Republic; and during his playing days in the 1960s and early '70s, Marichal had been every bit as dominating a pitcher as Martinez was in 1997. A power pitcher best remembered for his high leg kick during his pitching delivery, the "Dominican Dandy" had won 243 games during his Hall of Fame career. He won 20 games or more in a season six times, his 191 victories during the 1960s were the most by any pitcher during that decade, and he struck out over 2,300 batters. However, during his great career the Cy Young Award had eluded him; Marichal had been passed over by the voters every year.

At the awards ceremony, several hundred attendees watched Marichal hand the Cy Young Award to the National League's best pitcher. "You don't know what it means to me and all Dominicans to present this trophy to Pedro Martinez," he said as he handed the trophy to the young pitcher. "I know how hard he worked for this, because I worked for 16 years and never could achieve this."

Martinez then stunned the crowd by handing the trophy back to Marichal and telling the retired pitcher that he deserved to be the first man from the Dominican Republic to receive a Cy Young Award. "It is an honor for me to get this award from a man who deserved one but never got it," Martinez said. "It is a pleasure to present it to my man, my daddy, Juan Marichal. This belongs to you.

"We're going to take it with us and hand it to the country," Martinez continued as the crowd cheered.

Martinez later told reporters his award-winning 1997 season could not measure up to Marichal's 1968 statistics: a 26-9 record, a 2.43 earned run average, and 30 complete games in 38 starts. "I still think that [Marichal's numbers] are so good that it's going to be hard for any of us in our generation to achieve what he did," Martinez said. "I think that he really deserved it. When I looked at my numbers, the ERA is not as important as doing the things he did. Completing 30 games is not real. He should be the first [Dominican to win the Cy Young Award]."

Shortly after the award ceremony, Martinez and Marichal returned to the Dominican Republic together, bearing the Cy Young trophy.

The two pitchers like and respect each other. Marichal says he has followed Martinez's career since the younger man was a high-school student signed by the Los Angeles Dodgers in 1988. "I really like his style," Marichal told the *Boston Globe* early in 1998. "He's very aggressive. He's not afraid to pitch, in and out. I think that was my style. I loved to pitch inside. Pedro, he has no fear. He knows how to pitch, even at his age. Sometimes it takes longer to become a good pitcher, but he has improved every year. And he has a better change-up than the one I threw." In a *Sports Illustrated* article published during the first month of the 1998 season, Marichal noted, "He's such an intelligent pitcher, and he's afraid of nothing. . . . I don't think I ever threw that hard."

Current major-league players who have to bat or pitch against the superstar agree with Marichal that Martinez is something special. "His fastball is probably in the top five in baseball, his breaking ball is probably in the top 10, and his change-up is probably the best," Red Sox reliever Jim Corsi told *Sports Illustrated*. "You combine that with a great command of his pitches and just enough cockiness, and you get a guy who can throw any pitch, anytime, anywhere."

"He's the first person I've ever seen with an above-average fastball and an above-average change-up, too," noted another superstar pitcher, 1995 American League Cy Young Award–winner Randy Johnson. Jim Leyland, manager of the 1997 World Champion Florida Marlins, agreed: "He's not a good pitcher, he's a great pitcher." And even the best hitters know they're in for a tough at-bat when the hard-throwing right-hander is on the mound. "Pedro has the ability to throw every single one of his pitches for strikes," moaned Cleveland slugger David Justice. "Then you can't

Pedro Martinez waves to the crowd after striking out Florida Marlins' Kurt Abbott for his 300th strike out of the 1997 season at Olympic Stadium in Montreal, September 25, 1997.

help but respect his fastball." And veteran infielder Shawn Dunston noted: "Pedro is going to be a good one for years to come."

Martinez has become a hero to boys and girls in the baseball-crazy Dominican Republic. He is so popular in his native country that a national celebration was held when he won the Cy Young Award, and a labor strike was halted at his request. The slight-built pitcher provides good reasons for this love and respect. When he signed a six-year, $75 million contract with the Boston Red Sox—one of the richest baseball contracts ever—a few weeks after being named the Cy Young Award–winner for 1997, he donated money to build a church in his Dominican Republic hometown, Manoguayabo. The Immaculate Conception church, which sits on a hill surrounded by Manoguayabo's rough dirt roads and cinder-block houses, was dedicated on February 15, 1998, just a few hours before Martinez left for spring training with his new team. "That was better than the Cy Young [Award], better than the new contract," Martinez said. "The people mobbed me and hugged me. The priest blessed me. Everyone had tears in their eyes. It was unbelievable." In another article on the dedication, he commented, "I never got tears in my eyes when I won the Cy Young Award or when I win or lose a game. It was beautiful, the painting of the walls, the decorations. I didn't talk. I didn't touch anything. I felt realized. It was something I wanted to do long before I signed the contract." In addition to the steepled church, Martinez has also paid to construct a gymnasium and two baseball fields in his hometown, and he has had houses built for members of his family. The week before Christmas, Pedro and his brothers, along with Toronto Blue Jays pitcher Juan

Guzman, distributed presents to more than 1,000 children in Manoguayabo.

In a time when many of the most famous and well-paid athletes and entertainers rudely mistreat their fans, Pedro Martinez is an exception. He once told a reporter that he felt obligated to sign autographs. "It's an honor for me. It means some of those guys look at me as somebody really special. They just want to have my writing on a piece of paper." A spring 1998 visit to watch a young Dominican baseball player at Boston's Northeastern University reveals a lot about his character. "He said he remembered himself 10 years ago or so as a struggling Dominican player," Northeastern baseball coach Neal McPhee told Howard Ulman of the Associated Press. "He said he came to support a fellow countryman.

Pedro Martinez watches construction of the church he financed in his home town of Manoguayabo in the Dominican Republic.

"It made such a statement about who Pedro is. It was an incredible sight to see the biggest name in baseball being such a real person."

It is clear that Pedro Martinez has never forgotten humbler days, when he was growing up in one of the poorest nations in the world. But what Martinez has made equally clear with his breakthrough 1997 season—followed in 1998 by a 19-7 season in which he led the Red Sox to the American League playoffs—is that, although he's a nice person off the field, his kindness does not extend to anyone facing him with a bat in his hand.

CHAPTER TWO
Growing Up in the Dominican Republic

The Dominican Republic occupies the eastern two-thirds of the Caribbean island of Hispaniola, which it shares with the nation of Haiti. The island was discovered by Christopher Columbus in 1492, and the settlement that today is the Dominican Republic's capital city, Santo Domingo, was founded by Columbus's brother Bartholomew in 1496. It is the oldest continuously inhabited city in the Americas. The island was controlled first by the Spanish, then by the French, before independence was declared in 1821. However, the next 150 years in the Dominican Republic's history were troubled—it suffered armed invasions by both Spain and neighboring Haiti, periodic revolutions, and corrupt governments that plunged the country's economy into chaos. During World War I, the situation became so bad that the United States sent troops to occupy the country, using it as a strategic base to protect approaches to the Panama Canal. From 1930 to 1938, and again from 1942 to 1952 the island was ruled by a ruthless dictator, General Rafael Leónidas Trujillo Molina. Since his assassination in 1961, however, life on the island has remained relatively stable, though impoverished.

Today, about 7.5 million people live in the Dominican Republic. Most inhabitants live in the central part of the country, especially in the Cibao Valley and the Santo Domingo region. Most of the people speak Spanish and are Roman Catholic. The average resident of the Dominican Republic makes just $950 a year, and most of the jobs are in the fields harvesting sugarcane. Poverty has forced many people to leave the countryside and move into the towns, especially to Santo Domingo, but it is often difficult for the new urban dwellers to find employment. As a result, each year thousands of Dominicans choose to leave the country, seeking better lives in the United States and elsewhere.

Paulino and Laopoldina Martinez were one couple that had decided to remain in the Dominican Republic after a democratic government was installed with the death of the dictator Trujillo Molina. They already had four children—two sons and two daughters—when Laopoldina gave birth to a third son, whom they named Pedro, on October 25, 1971. Pedro was born in a hospital in Santo Domingo, but he was taken a few days later to the family home in Manoguayabo, a rural town with about 1,000 residents where the main jobs are in the sugarcane fields. The Martinez family had a small two-acre *finca* (farm), and Paulino worked as a janitor at the local school.

The most popular sport in the Dominican Republic is baseball. In fact, it is more than just a game there, it's a national obsession. In the two decades before Pedro Martinez was born, a constant stream of talented Hispanic baseball players began to make their way into the major leagues. Many of these came from the Dominican Republic, including brothers Felipe, Matty, and Jesus Alou and pitcher Juan Marichal. By 1997, 9.74 percent of all major-league players came from the Dominican Republic, a figure surpassed only by California (15.26 percent).

Paulino Martinez himself was a pretty good pitcher for various adult teams before he started his family; he played on various winter-league teams alongside the Alou brothers in the 1960s, and Felipe Alou once said that he could have pitched in the major leagues. "I was too poor to leave the country," Paulino later explained. "When the Giants invited me for a tryout, I didn't have cleats. So I couldn't go to the tryout." As each of his children grew older, he taught them how to play baseball and encouraged them to practice. "Baseball is in my family," Pedro said. "It's in my blood."

Pedro and his brothers and sisters grew up without much money. After the birth of Pedro's brother Jesus, there were eight people living in a small house that did not even have a toilet. The Martinez family could not afford to buy baseball equipment; instead, the brothers practiced with whatever they could find, playing ball in vacant lots or in the streets. Pedro used broomsticks as bats and oranges, rolled-up socks, and rocks as balls to practice his hitting. He even took the heads off his sisters' dolls to use as balls.

"When my sisters came home from school, they'd find them with no head and they would go, 'Mommy! Mommy!'" he said. "I would take anything that was round to play baseball. That's the passion I had."

Although the family did not have a lot of money, Pedro's childhood was mostly happy. However, when he was nine years old, his parents decided that they could no longer live together and ended their marriage. Pedro coped with the stress of his parents' divorce with the help of his brothers, especially 13-year-old Ramon. "Our parents cared for us and did a great job instilling values in us," Pedro told Boston sportswriter Peter Gammons in 1998. "But Ramon is the biggest reason I have gotten where I am. He is the great one in this family. I am still Ramon's little brother." In 1997 he told USA Today. "[Ramon] has taught me a lot of things. One is that you have to remember to work hard. Two, he showed me how to get my frustrations out. He said to me, 'Take it out by running, so you don't snap.' I do that and it works. He also taught me to appreciate everything that I have. And I try to do that every day."

Both Ramon and Nelson Martinez, who was a year younger than Ramon, were good baseball players: Ramon a pitcher, Nelson an infielder who was good enough to be invited to a tryout by the Pittsburgh Pirates (he injured his knee and never played in the majors). Pedro looked up to his older siblings and shared their love for the sport. "Ever since I know I'm alive, I played baseball," he said. "I played anywhere, in any little room we had, the backyard, the house. I'd accidentally hit people, playing in the streets. I'd even quit school to play baseball. I'd tell my mom I was going to school, then run into a friend on the way, and my time for school would be over."

By the time Ramon was 15, he had developed into an excellent pitcher. A Los Angeles Dodgers' scout named Ralph Avila took an interest in the gangly teen, and he invited him to a special tryout camp, where Ramon learned the nuances of pitching. After that, Ramon was invited to join an amateur baseball team, the Manoguayabo Braves. Pedro was 11 at the time, and he often walked from town to town—sometimes three miles away—just to watch his brother pitch. By 1984, 16-year-old Ramon was good enough to be selected as a member of the Dominican Republic's national baseball team, which competed in the Olympic Games in Los Angeles. He pitched three scoreless innings against Taiwan. Three weeks after the Olympics, the Dodgers offered Ramon a minor-league contract—the first step toward the major leagues.

As Ramon began working out in the Dodgers' minor-league system, playing for their farm team in the Dominican Republic, Pedro followed his brother to games, carrying his equipment bag. "Just to see professional ballplayers in the Dominican was special, but to be on the same field was a dream," he said years later. "I used to dream that one day, my brothers and I would be in the major leagues together."

It seemed unlikely. Although he had a "live" arm—a term used by baseball scouts and coaches when talking about someone who throws the ball hard—at under 6 feet tall and just 150 pounds Pedro seemed too frail to survive the rigors of the long baseball season. But before one of Ramon's games, Dodgers scouts noticed that their starting pitcher was throwing warmup tosses with his little brother. They trained a radar gun on Pedro and were surprised to find that the skinny 15-year-old right-hander was throwing the ball 80 mph. The Dodgers offered him a professional contract, which Pedro signed a year later, on June 18, 1988. He felt like his dreams were coming true. That same year, Ramon Martinez made his major-league debut with the Dodgers, and L.A.'s newest prospect hoped that one day, he too would pitch in Dodger Stadium.

CHAPTER THREE
The Road to the Major Leagues

It's not easy for a baseball player to make it to the major leagues from the Dominican Republic—or from anywhere else, for that matter. Young professional baseball players typically must work their way through four minor-league levels: rookie ball, Class A, Class AA, and Class AAA. Each time a player moves to a new level, he finds the competition is tougher. A player may be able to get away with making some mistakes in rookie-league ball; however, by the time he reaches Triple-A, any flaws in his game—such as an inability to hit the curve ball or a lack of control when pitching—will keep that player from ever reaching the majors. In fact, many players who are talented still aren't good enough to be promoted from their first rookie team. Joe McIlvaine, a former scout for the Baltimore Orioles, California Angels, and Milwaukee Brewers, recalled his years looking for prospects in the Dominican Republic in Mike Bryan's 1989 book *Baseball Lives:*

> I would go to every little outpost I could find with Eddie Toledo, our man in the Dominican Republic; we would have [tryout] camps at every field and condition imaginable. One time we went to have a tryout camp and there was a little student uprising down the street. The police came out to quell the semi-riot with tear gas and all the tear gas floated onto our field and we had to call off our workout because all our players got tear-gassed. Just another day at the yard in Santo Domingo.... We signed a

lot of players, but the success rate of all the players signed in the Dominican is probably 2 percent.

Pedro (left) his first year with the Dodgers

When Pedro signed his contract with the Dodgers in June 1988, he immediately reported to their rookie team in Santo Domingo, where he played for the final two months of the season. He was an instant success at Santo

Domingo. Martinez appeared in eight games, starting seven, and compiled a 5-1 record. One of his victories was a complete game. He gave up just 45 hits and 25 runs (17 earned) for a 3.12 ERA, while striking out 28 batters and walking 16.

While Pedro's achievements in his first year of professional baseball were significant, they were somewhat overshadowed by the exploits of his older brother Ramon. After three and a half seasons in the minor leagues, the Dodgers called Ramon up to the major leagues for the last two months of the 1988 season, and he made his big-league debut on August 13. Ramon earned his first win in a Dodgers' uniform on August 29; he finished the season with a 1-3 mark and a 3.78 ERA in the majors. After that experience, Ramon promised himself that he would do better in the majors next season, while Pedro just hoped he could duplicate his brother's success in passing through the Dodgers' minor-league system to make the main club.

The next season, Pedro seemed to be on track to achieve that goal. In 1989 he returned to Santo Domingo and went from being a good prospect to a dominant pitcher. Appearing in 13 games, he improved his record to 7-2 and lowered his ERA to 2.75. He pitched a pair of complete-game shutouts in his seven starts, and he earned one save in his six relief appearances. Most importantly, Pedro showed that he was becoming a better pitcher, gaining control of his blazing fastball and off-speed pitches. He allowed fewer hits per inning, giving up just 59 hits in the $85^2/3$ innings he pitched, and he walked fewer batters per game while increasing his strikeouts per outing. He struck out 63 batters and walked just 25, for a strikeout-walk ratio of 2.52-1, a significant improvement over the 1.75-1 that he had posted in his first season.

His excellent rookie-league statistics over his first year and a half in professional baseball caused the Dodgers to move Pedro Martinez up to the next level in rookie-league ball. He was assigned to a team in the United States, Great Falls, for the 1990 season. Martinez responded well to the move to a tougher league: he started 14 games, won eight and lost three, and recorded a 3.62 earned run average. In the 77 innings he pitched, he struck out 82 batters—better than one strikeout an inning.

While Pedro was toiling in the low minors, Ramon was having a breakthrough season with the Dodgers. In 1989 Ramon Martinez had played half the season for Los Angeles' Class AAA team, Albuquerque, and the other half with the major-league club, where he compiled a 6-4 record and a 3.18 ERA in 15 appearances. In 1990 he made the Dodgers team in spring training. He had a phenomenal rookie season, going 20-6 with a 2.92 ERA. At age 22, Ramon became the youngest pitcher in Dodgers history to win 20 games in a season. He also led the major leagues with 12 complete games and ranked second in the National League in victories, strikeouts (223 in 234 innings), and complete-game shutouts (3). Ramon's best month was June: on June 4 he struck out 18 Atlanta Braves to tie a Dodgers record, and his 4-0 record and 1.76 ERA for the month earned him the National League's Player of the Month award. He was selected to the NL All-Star team and was runner-up to Doug Drabek of the Pittsburgh Pirates in the voting for the National League's Cy Young Award.

The Dodger brass was excited about their new pitching star, and they felt good enough about his younger brother Pedro that they promoted him to their Class-A team, the Bakersfield Blaze in the California League, for the 1991 season. Pedro Martinez knew the step from rookie

Pedro's older brother Ramon was one of the Dodgers' best pitchers in 1990 and 1991; here he hurls the ball to the plate during a July 1991 game against the San Diego Padres.

ball to Single-A would be an important one. The 19-year-old had worked out hard in the off-season, and the results of his preparation were apparent. He was unbeaten at 8-0 in the 10 starts that he made for Bakersfield in the early months of the 1991 season. Single-A hitters could scarcely touch Martinez's pitches: his earned run average was a scintillating 2.05 and he struck out 83 batters in 61 $1/2$ innings while walking just 19.

Because of this fine performance, the Dodgers decided to move him up to the next level, Class AA San Antonio in the Texas League, in midseason 1991. While his won-lost record with the Missions was just 7-5, Martinez allowed only 1.76 earned runs per nine innings and struck out 74 batters in 76 $2/3$ innings. He completed four of his 12 starts and pitched three shutouts.

While he was with the Missions, another member of the San Antonio squad gave Pedro a book of biographies and statistics of some of baseball's greatest players.

As he paged through the book, he paid special attention to the histories of players from the Dominican Republic. He was particularly interested in the accomplishments of a pitcher named Juan Antonio Sanchez Marichal. Marichal had won 20 games in a season six times, had a career winning percentage of .631, and had struck out over 2,300 batters. Surprised that Marichal had never won the Cy Young Award, Martinez made a vow that he recalled to the Associated Press in 1997:"I said to myself that if I ever made it and became something good, that I would dedicate something to Juan."

Although the day that he would pitch at the major-league level was still a few years away, Martinez knew he was getting closer. The Dodgers' minor-league administrators recognized that the team's young prospect was obviously not overmatched at either Class A or AA, so they decided to move Pedro up again before the 1991 season was over. They promoted him to Triple-A Albuquerque—one step away from the major leagues—with just over a month left in the season. He started six games for the Albuquerque Dukes, recording a 3-3 record, a 3.66 ERA, and 35 strikeouts in $39^1/3$ innings.

The next year, 1992, Martinez was given a full year at Albuquerque, and he did his best to prove that he was ready for the big leagues. In 20 starts, he went 7-6 with a 3.81 ERA, three complete games, and a shutout. He struck out a team-leading 124 batters (third in the Pacific Coast League) and allowed just 104 hits in $125^1/3$ innings. His successful season led to his selection for the Triple-A All-Star Game, and *Baseball America* named him the 10th-best major-league prospect and the third-best prospect in the PCL in an annual poll of the top 100 minor-league players. But for Pedro, the most important event of the 1992 season was when the Dodgers called him up to join his older brother in the big club for the final month of the year.

On September 24, 1992, Pedro Martinez made his major-league debut, starting for the Dodgers against the Cincinnati Reds. He pitched seven innings but did not earn a decision, allowing a run and striking out seven batters. He appeared in relief in his second Dodgers game a few days later, but he gave up a run and lost the game. His final statistics for his first major-league appearance were an 0-1 record, 8 innings pitched, 8 strikeouts and 1 walk, and a 2.25 ERA.

Pedro was thrilled to be in the major leagues and pleased to join his older brother on the Dodgers' pitching staff. In his second and third major-league seasons, Ramon had continued to be one of the team's best pitchers, leading Los Angeles with 17 wins in 1991 and winning eight games before an arm injury ended his 1992 season.

Pedro was having some arm troubles himself. Fortunately, however, the injury was to his left arm, not his pitching arm. In the off-season, Pedro underwent surgery to correct the arm soreness. The surgery was successful, and after a rehabilitation period he focused on getting back into shape. His goal: to make the team in spring training 1993.

CHAPTER FOUR
The Major Leagues

W hen the Los Angeles Dodgers opened their spring training at Vero Beach in February 1993, Pedro Martinez hoped that he could perform well enough to make the big-league club's roster for opening day, April 1. He had been training in the months since his post-1992 season arm surgery, and he felt confident that he was ready to face major-league hitters.

However, although he pitched effectively in spring training, Dodgers manager Tommy Lasorda decided that Ramon Martinez's younger brother should return to Triple-A to start the season. Pedro hid his disappointment, packed his bags, and returned to Albuquerque.

He would not remain in a Dukes uniform long. Pedro made just one appearance at Albuquerque, starting the team's first game of the season. He struck out four batters in the first three innings; then pitching coach Dave Wallace came to the mound. "Pretend your arm hurts," Wallace told him. "I've got to get you out of this game. You're going to L.A." When Pedro reached Los Angeles, the Dodgers assigned him to a relief role in the team's bullpen. Pedro Martinez was in the big leagues to stay.

In his first major-league appearance of 1993, Pedro relieved his brother Ramon. This marked the first time that brothers pitched for the same team in the same game since 1979, when Rick and Mickey Mahler pitched together for the Atlanta Braves. On May 5, Pedro earned his first major-league win in relief against the New York Mets.

As the 1993 season went on, the rookie reliever began to draw attention as an up-and-coming star for the

Dodgers. Between May 25 and August 6, he won eight consecutive decisions. By the end of the season, he had appeared in a Dodgers rookie record 65 games, racking up a

10-5 record with two saves and a 2.61 earned run average. His 10 victories led all National League relievers and was third best among NL rookie pitchers, and his 119 strikeouts were third best among rookie pitchers in the major leagues that year. Opposing batters found Martinez's offerings difficult to hit. They managed just a .201 batting average as he allowed only 76 hits over 107 innings and stranded 26 of 33 inherited runners. His pitching helped the Dodgers improve from a last-place finish in 1992 to third in the National League West in '93.

Despite Pedro's excellent rookie season, and the fact that he had been successful in the two starts he made for Los Angeles in 1993, the Dodgers did not feel confident that the skinny young pitcher—just 5-foot-11 and 160 pounds—had the size and stamina to be a successful starter in the major leagues. (At 6-foot-4 and 190 pounds, Ramon was significantly bigger.) "Everybody at Dodger stadium used to say, 'Hey, who are you?,'" Pedro recalled. "I'd say, 'I'm the batboy.' They'd say, 'There's your gate over there.' I'd follow the joke. I didn't mind."

In 1993 when this photo was taken, Pedro was an up-and-coming rookie relief pitcher.

Los Angeles also felt that it needed to upgrade its infield both offensively and defensively in order to compete for the NL West title. On November 19, 1993, the Dodgers traded Pedro to the Montreal Expos for second baseman Delino DeShields, a career .277 hitter who had batted over .289 in three of four seasons with the Expos. Pedro was sorry to leave the Dodgers, the team that had given him a start in professional baseball, and disappointed that he would not be pitching on the same staff as his brother. But the Expos' pitching staff was not very strong, and the trade would be an excellent opportunity for the young pitcher.

Martinez was moving to a team with a history much different than that of the Dodgers. The Montreal Expos have never been particularly popular in Canada, where ice hockey is the national sport. Because the Expos play in a small market, they can not afford to pay large salaries to retain their good players. Typically, they trade their best players for lower-priced prospects (DeShields' 1994 salary with the Dodgers would be more than 10 times the $200,000 the Expos would pay Martinez), rather than lose them for nothing to free agency. As a result, the Expos always seem to be a young, rebuilding team.

Montreal has never won even a regular-season pennant. In 1979 the team finished two games out of first place in the NL East; the next year, the Philadelphia Phillies defeated the Expos in the last game of the season to snatch the division crown. In the strike-shortened 1981 season, the Expos won their only division title, racking up the best record in the National League during the second half of the season, but they lost the National League Championship Series in five games to the Dodgers. The franchise was moderately competitive during the rest of the 1980s—

usually finishing in the middle of the NL East pack—but had fallen on hard times by 1991, when the team finished at the bottom of the East standings with a 71-91 record. Adding to the frustration, the Expos had to play the last month of the '91 season on the road after a large chunk of concrete fell out of the roof of Montreal's Olympic Stadium.

But the Expos seemed to be on an upswing after hiring Felipe Alou as the team's manager on May 22, 1992. Alou, who like Pedro Martinez had grown up in the Dominican Republic, had a stellar 17-year playing career with the San Francisco Giants and Milwaukee Braves, during which he batted .286 with over 2,000 hits and 200 home runs and was named to the All-Star team three times. He played briefly for the Expos at the end of his career in 1973, then was a coach and manager in the Expos organization for almost two decades. Alou's 1992 squad surprised many baseball observers by finishing second in the NL East with 87 wins. The next year, the Expos improved to a 94-68 mark, one victory shy of matching the team's single-season record, and remained in the hunt for the 1993 NL East crown until the final week of the season.

Outfielders Larry Walker, Marquis Grissom, and the manager's son Moises Alou provided offensive punch in Montreal's lineup, but the Expos manager knew that, in order to win in 1994, he would need improved starting pitching. Jeff Fassero and Ken Hill were expected to lead the pitching staff. Hill, a six-year veteran, had won 16 games with the Expos in 1992 and gone 9-7 in '93. Fassero had pitched well in relief in 1992 (8-7, with a 2.68 ERA in 70 appearances), and then split time between starting and bullpen duty in 1993, compiling a 12-5 record and a 2.30

ERA in 56 games. Alou was counting on him as a full-time starter in 1994.

Before the start of the season, Alou and Montreal pitching coach Joe Kerrigan discussed the role they wanted Pedro Martinez to play on their pitching staff. Both felt that Martinez had the tools—an explosive fastball complemented by a change-up and curveball—to be either a dominant relief pitcher or an excellent starter. Because it is difficult to find major-league-quality starting pitchers, Kerrigan and Alou decided to groom their young pitcher for a starting role. "There was a lot of skepticism because of his size and frame, but we figured he could start," Kerrigan told *USA Today* reporter Mel Antonen in 1998. "The reason? Three great pitches."

In 1994 Pedro Martinez would get what he had been hoping for: an opportunity to prove that he could start in the major leagues.

Fellow Dominican Felipe Alou recognized Pedro's talent at an early age.

CHAPTER FIVE
Señor Plunk

Montreal manager Felipe Alou once said that a reason he decided to make Pedro Martinez a starter before the 1994 season was because the young Dominican reminded him of three great pitchers Alou had played against in the 1960s: Juan Marichal, Bob Gibson, and Don Drysdale. Like Martinez, all three were tough, determined right-handers who weren't afraid to blaze a fastball inside to back hitters off the plate.

"He's similar to Juan Marichal, along the lines of presentation—fearless and challenging," Alou told *USA Today.* "He's a young, skinny kid throwing 95-mile-per-hour fastballs inside on the plate. Batters don't like that. You have to be tough. If you're small, you've got to be tougher."

In his first season with the Expos, the slender hurler set out to show the league he could be as tough as any pitcher. At times, it seemed, Martinez pitched as though the inside of the plate belonged to him exclusively—a sentiment National League batters didn't appreciate. He whistled a lot of high-and-inside fastballs past the hands of hitters and hit a league-leading 11 batters. In his 23 starts, there were three fights, with 12 players ejected for fighting, charging the mound, or hitting Montreal batters in retaliation.

Soon, Martinez's reputation as a bean-ball pitcher—he was labeled Señor Plunk by sportswriters—had gotten so bad that umpires were issuing warnings to the young pitcher in the first inning, or whenever he would lose his grip on a curveball. Alou maintained that Martinez was doing nothing wrong and was still learning the game.

"It's an injustice to sign a 16-year-old from the Dominican Republic because he's not as physically mature as a 16-year-old from North America," Alou said. "We're not being honest if we expect him to know everything right off the bat. He's just a wild kid, a baby. It takes a little longer."

The situation culminated in a 1994 meeting between Martinez, Alou, Montreal pitching coach Kerrigan, and NL president Len Coleman. Four years later, Kerrigan recalled, "Felipe said that Pedro was a young man who was a tremendous positive for baseball and that we should be thinking of him in a positive image instead of a negative light. The perception was horrible for Pedro. He wasn't a headhunter. After that meeting, it helped. Umpires got the message that if he was throwing inside, sometimes it was because of a mechanical flaw."

Despite the controversy over Pedro's inside pitching, his first season as a starter was successful. He finished with an 11-5 record and a 3.42 ERA, striking out 142 batters in 144 innings. He pitched a complete-game shutout and also made one relief appearance, earning a save, in contributing to the Expos' best season ever. Montreal had plowed over the rest of the National League, compiling a record of 74-40 on August 11. Montreal's .649 winning percentage was the best in major-league baseball, even though the team had just two players over 30 on the squad and the third-lowest payroll in the major leagues. The Expos seemed to be a lock to go to the NL playoffs for the first time since 1981, and there were hopes that Montreal could reach the World Series for the first time in team history.

Unfortunately, on August 12 the Major League Players Association went on strike, canceling the last 52 days of the 1994 season. The strike marked the first time since 1904 that the World Series was not held. The premature end to the Expos' fine season was a great disappointment to Montreal fans.

Alou was recognized for the Expos' outstanding performance by being named Major League Manager of the Year by the Associated Press and National League Manager of the Year by the *Sporting News*. But the veteran skipper knew that if the strike ended, he would have a harder time keeping the Expos competitive during the 1995 season. As usual, Montreal traded its three highest-paid players to other teams during the off-season, receiving minor-league prospects in exchange. As a result, they dumped a total of about $10.1 million in salary, but they lost Walker (.322 average and 19 home runs), Grissom (96 runs scored in 110 games), and Hill (16-5 record, 3.32 ERA).

Because of the strike, the start of the 1995 season was delayed by nearly a month, and the regular season was cut from 162 games to 144. Martinez knew that with the trade of former staff ace Hill to St. Louis a few weeks before the opener, he would have an excellent opportunity to claim the top spot in the rotation in 1995. He proved to Alou and to Montreal fans that he was up to the challenge, going 14-10 with a 3.51 ERA, leading the team in victories and placing fifth in the league in wins and strikeouts (174). He allowed a stingy .227 batting average, allowing just 158 hits in his 194 2/3 innings, and threw a pair of complete-game shutouts. Martinez's accomplishment was all the more impressive because the inexperienced Expos squad was having trouble scoring runs, falling to a record of 74-88. One night in June was a perfect example of how the Expos' lack of offensive punch affected Martinez's won-lost record: he pitched nine perfect innings on June 3 against the San Diego Padres, not allowing a hit or a walk, but

Montreal couldn't score either and lost the game in the 10th.

National League batters still complained because Martinez continued to pitch inside, and there were several problems during the year. Pedro received three early-season warnings for allegedly throwing at batters' heads, was fined $500 for plunking Houston's Luis Gonzalez, and finished tied for third in the league with 11 hit batters.

Sometimes Pedro miscalculates a throw and hits the batters. This earned him the nickname Señor Plunk early in his career.

"I don't come inside to hurt anybody," Pedro would explain to Ray Glier in 1997. "I come inside to pitch. That's what I'm doing. I'm looking for the best way for me to succeed. If I do it with a good fastball, it's got to be in. If I leave it away, they'll hit it three miles out of the park. They are strong. They will hit it. No matter how hard you throw it, they will hit it."

The next season Pedro solidified his position as one of the best up-and-coming pitchers in the National League. He threw the best game of his major-league career to date, a two-hit shutout against the New York Mets in Shea Stadium on May 1, then struck out 11 batters during a four-hit shutout of Cincinnati on June 14. As a result, Atlanta Braves manager

Bobby Cox selected him as a member of the National League All-Star team pitching staff.

The right-hander may have been a little nervous as he walked to the mound to start the sixth inning of the All-Star Game. He gave up a pair of singles and a walk to load the bases, an uncharacteristic start, but then settled down to retire the next three batters and escape the inning without allowing a run. His outing preserved a shutout for the National League All-Stars, who won the game 6-0.

One of the most important games of Pedro's season occurred on August 29, when he faced big brother Ramon and the Dodgers. Both brothers were masterful. Ramon pitched eight innings, struck out seven batters, and allowed just three hits and one run. Pedro struck out 12 and walked one, pitching his fourth complete game of the season. Unfortunately, he made two mistakes in the fourth inning, and Los Angeles' Mike Piazza and Eric Karros responded by hitting both mistakes out of the park. Pedro and the Expos lost by a 2-1 score.

"I'm very proud of the job that [Pedro] did," Ramon commented after the game. "It was a big challenge for both of us. When he left the mound in the ninth, I made a sign to him to tell him that I love him and that he pitched a great game. Neither of us wanted to give it up and that's the way it should be. I don't feel sorry. I feel very proud of him. It could have been him the winner and me the loser. I have pitched better games and I've been in other good duels, but this is different. It was a big challenge."

His battery mate, Dodgers catcher Mike Piazza, agreed. "It was a big game and a big win for us. . . . If anything, I think Ramon was more serious than usual. I didn't notice much joking from either of them. It was business out there. It was a gutsy and aggressive game from both of them and it must have been exciting for the brothers."

Pedro was gracious in defeat, and complimentary toward his older brother. "He's been a great example to me as a person and as a player my whole life," he said. "I look up to him and he's always been there for me. He taught me how to play baseball and he's taught me about life. He's my idol. It was a little different preparing for this game because I had to go up there thinking that I was going to defeat my brother or that he was going to defeat me. It was hard and it will never be easy if it happens again, because it's blood against blood and it's the same blood."

Pedro (right) with agent, Fernando Cuza

Between 1995 and '96, Martinez had bettered nearly every aspect of his game, but especially notable was his improved control. As the '96 season drew to a close, he had hit just two batters all season. But his control troubles returned in a game September 24 against the Philadelphia Phillies when he plunked outfielder Gregg Jefferies in the back. When the Expos' ace took his turn at bat, Phillies hurler Mike Williams threw at Martinez twice in retaliation. The slender pitcher angrily dropped his bat and charged the mound, sparking a brawl.

The National League responded to the incident by suspending Martinez for his last appearance of the 1996 season and for the first seven games of the 1997 season. Alou protested the ruling bitterly. "He was allowed to be thrown at twice," the Montreal manager argued. "He has the right to defend himself."

Despite this incident, it was a very solid season for Martinez, who again led the Expos in victories. His 13-10 record might have been better but for the ineptitude of the inexperienced Montreal offense, which scored just 22 runs in his 10 losses. Martinez set career highs in innings pitched (216.2), strikeouts (222), and complete games (4); his earned run average was 3.70. The team itself had made great strides from 1995, finishing in second place in the NL East with an 88-74 record and remaining in the hunt for a wild-card playoff spot until the last two weeks of the season.

Pedro went back to the Dominican Republic during the off-season, resolved to work hard and pitch even better in his fourth full major-league campaign. The 1997 season that was to come would be beyond even his wildest imaginings.

Pedro with his Aunt Gloria

CHAPTER SIX
A Breakthrough Season

Because of his late-1996 suspension, Martinez was not allowed to appear in the Expos' first seven games of 1997. His first scheduled start, April 10 against St. Louis, was postponed because of snow. As a result, he did not take his first turn on the mound until April 15, two weeks after the season started.

For Expos fans, it was worth the wait. Martinez scattered three hits over six innings, striking out five batters and allowing one run in a 7-5 win over the Houston Astros. His next two starts were shutout victories over the Padres and Mets, leaving him with a 3-0 record and a scintillating 0.44 ERA.

"He really shows his command of pitching now," Alou remarked after the Mets game. "He's on a mission. There's no more talk about him pitching up-and-in when it comes to Pedro. He's going to be one of the best in the league this year."

Martinez seemed to be on track to fulfill Alou's prediction. In his next start, May 1 against the Astros, he tossed a three-hit shutout, striking out nine batters, then followed up with a seven-inning performance against the San Francisco Giants in which he struck out 10 batters and allowed just two hits. He gave up a run in the fifth inning—just the second he had allowed all season—as he improved to 5-0. In his next outing, a complete-game victory against San Diego on May 13, he allowed two earned runs and struck out seven San Diego batters while walking none. That sixth victory tied Ken Hill's team record for consecutive wins to start a season—a mark he broke in his next start. Pedro's seventh win of the season was particularly sweet, as it came against the Dodgers. In his first career win against his former team, Martinez struck out seven and contributed offensively with a base hit and a run scored.

The 1997 Cy Young Award winner is also a charitable player, contributing much to his homeland, the Dominican Republic.

Pedro became the first National League pitcher that year to win eight games on May 23 with a 4-1 decision over the Pirates. In his third complete game of the season, he matched his career high with 12 strikeouts and lowered his league-leading earned-run average to 1.17. Reporters were beginning to compare him to the American League's leading pitchers—Toronto's Roger Clemens and Baltimore's Jimmy Key, each with eight victories—but Martinez downplayed the comparison to the two former Cy Young Award–winners. "I can't compete with those guys," he told the Associated Press. "They're older and more experienced. They've proven they're better than me. I've got to keep working and keep my feet on the ground. That's a pretty big compliment. . . . I just hope God keeps me healthy and I'll keep trying to do it every five days."

The right-hander's incredible start had erased all talk of head-hunting. In a *Baseball Weekly* article, Martinez attributed his improved control to maturity. "I'm still learning, but I feel like I have a better idea," he said. "As time goes on and if I don't do good and I keep hitting people, then, maybe, people can talk about me [as a headhunter]. But as I am improving, so are my chances for respect."

Pedro's battery mate, Montreal catcher Darrin Fletcher, agreed. "He was young and I think the veteran hitters were trying to intimidate him into not [pitching inside] anymore," Fletcher said in the *Baseball Weekly* article. "They were basically trying to say, 'I don't want you to pitch it in there, I want it out over the plate so I can hit a double.'

"Over time as he has established himself in the league, hitters have submitted to his wishes. They know for a fact he is going to pitch up and in and that you never know if that ball is going to whistle in up by your hands. I think that's an asset—hitters are becoming too comfortable in the box."

Pedro's victory string ended in his next start. The Mets scored five unearned runs en route to a 7-0 victory— the team's first against Martinez in 15 career appearances. New York mound ace Bobby Jones moved ahead of Martinez in the victory column with his ninth win of the year. Five days later, again pitching against Jones and the Mets, Martinez allowed just two earned runs, scattering seven hits and striking out 12 batters. But New York prevailed again, 2-1. The loss dropped Martinez's record to 8-2.

Against the Chicago Cubs on June 8, Martinez set a new career high with 13 strikeouts, but he didn't figure in the decision. He surpassed his personal-best strikeout total in the next game, fanning 14 Detroit Tigers in a three-hit, complete-game shutout that extended a Montreal winning streak to eight games. Martinez struck out 12 more in a complete game against Florida on June 20, but the Marlins won 2-1 to take a two-game lead over the Expos in the race for second in the NL East. Florida catcher Charles Johnson drove in both Florida runs with a solo home run in the sixth inning and a seventh-inning RBI triple.

On June 30, Martinez and the Expos faced Canada's other baseball team, the Toronto Blue Jays. The crowd of 37,430 at Toronto's SkyDome was treated to a great pitching duel between the Expos' ace and 1996 Cy Young Award–winner Pat Hentgen. Behind a masterful performance by Martinez—he threw a complete game, didn't allow a hit until the sixth inning, and struck out 10 Jays—the Expos won the interleague contest, 2-1.

Pedro's string of dominating performances led him to be selected for the National League's All-Star team for the second straight year. But in his final start before the midseason break, Martinez was roughed up by the league's best team, the Atlanta Braves. The 5-3 loss, in a battle against fellow All-Star Tom Glavine, dropped his record to 10-4, and his ERA, though still best in the NL, rose from 1.54 to 1.74.

Despite the rocky outing against the Braves, Atlanta manager Bobby Cox, directing the 1997 NL All-Star team, called on Martinez to pitch the sixth inning of the game at Cleveland's Jacob's Field three days later. The slender right-hander proved up to the task with a perfect appearance. He retired three of the American League's most dangerous hitters, striking out long-ball threat Alex Rodriguez and AL home-run leader Mark McGwire, then retiring Ken Griffey Jr., the league's second-leading home-run hitter, on a fly ball. However, the American League won the game, 3-1.

His first start after the break, against the Cincinnati Reds, came on a brutally hot day when temperatures on the field reached 110°F. Martinez, however, came to throw heat, not to be bothered by it. He allowed just one hit and struck out nine batters in his eighth complete game and third shutout of the season, a 2-0 Expos victory that improved his record to 11-4. Only one Cincinnati player reached second base during the game.

"It was terrible," Martinez said of the heat after the game. "Thank God I'm used to that weather. Coming from the Dominican, I'm used to it. When I got out there, right before the first pitch, I knew it was hot."

"He's dominant," said Alou. "Just another typical performance for him. He had a good curve, a good change-up, and an outstanding fastball. We asked him in the seventh [about the heat]. He said, 'Hey, I'm not sweating much.' I guess when you're in command like that, you don't really sweat that much."

"He's the closest thing I've seen to a perfect pitcher," Reds manager Ray Knight agreed after the game. "We got one hit, and it was a jam job. He had a dominating fastball and he has a good presence on the mound. He's something special."

Martinez had another good outing in his next start July 18 against the Astros but lost despite allowing just two runs and striking out nine batters in seven innings. The loss was another case of the Expos' being unable to provide run support when their ace was on the mound. Including this loss, the team had managed just 18 runs in Pedro's previous 10 starts, and he had lost five times. "I've got to try to win with what they give me," Martinez told the Associated Press. "I know they're trying hard. Believe me, this is not the type of team that's going to stay on the same pace all the time. I know they're going to break out of it and start scoring runs for me."

Martinez himself seemed to run out of gas in his next start, a 10-5 loss to the red-hot Astros, who were on a six-game winning streak. Pedro retired nine of the first 10 batters he faced but wound up allowing five runs in six innings; however, he did not figure in the decision. Five days later he rebounded with a five-hit shutout of the Colorado Rockies. This day, his fastball was deadly accurate once again—he struck out 13 Rockies and walked just one as he lowered his ERA to 1.80. He followed with another outstanding effort on August 3, a three-hitter to beat the Padres 7-3. Only one of the runs he gave up was earned, and Martinez also helped the team offensively by going 2 for 3 and scoring a run. On August 9 he pitched his third consecutive complete game—and league-leading 11th overall—defeating San Francisco 2-1. He allowed just four hits and struck out eight batters. With his 14th win of the season, he matched his career high, set in 1995. "I feel really focused now," Martinez commented afterward. "I know what it takes to stay focused. I hope I still remember it later on in the year."

The game was especially notable for Martinez as the Expos celebrated Latino Night at Olympic Stadium. The national anthem of the Dominican Republic was played before the game, along with the Canadian and U.S. anthems, and he had an opportunity to meet with Hall of Famer Juan Marichal, who threw out the first ball of the game.

As the season drew into deep August, the Expos' offensive woes continued. Pedro allowed just five hits and struck out 12 Dodgers, but catcher Mike Piazza's home run gave Los Angeles a 1-0 win on August 14. Then, on August 20, Martinez struck out 13 Cardinals—including seven in a row from the fourth through sixth innings, tying the Expos' 25-year-old club record set by Steve Renko—and didn't allow an earned run in $6^2/3$ innings, but Montreal errors led to a 6-3 loss.

With just about a month remaining in the 1997 season, the right-hander had a 15-6 record and was second in the National League with 245 strikeouts. He seemed to be getting stronger as the season progressed, striking out 69 batters in his last 47 innings, and baseball observers realized he had a good chance of becoming one of the few pitchers to strike out 300 batters in a season. In fact, only 12 other pitchers had ever whiffed that many hitters—a list that included such Hall of Famers as Steve Carlton, Sandy Kofax, and Nolan Ryan.

Pedro won his 16th game of the season in spectacular style, overpowering the American League's best team, the New York Yankees, in an interleague game, 7-2. After allowing a leadoff single to Yankee shortstop Derek Jeter, he retired 21 of the next 22 batters. His 252nd strikeout of the year, against Bernie Williams to open the seventh inning, broke an Expos record that had been set by Bill Stoneman in 1971—the year Pedro was born. He would strike out three more batters before completing his 12th game of the season.

With a month left in the season, the race for the league's Cy Young Award was heating up. Other top candidates included Atlanta's Denny Neagle and the nearly unhittable Greg Maddux; Philadelphia's Curt Schilling; and Houston ace Darryl Kile. But although Martinez had fewer wins than these pitchers, he had also been nearly unhittable, excelling despite weak offensive support.

"The numbers will talk," said Martinez. "I don't have to say anything about myself, Maddux, Neagle—anybody fighting for the Cy Young [Award]. All they have to do is look at the numbers and pick whoever they think deserves it."

Martinez struck out 11 Phillies in his next start, despite being hampered by a strained thumb ligament, but catcher Bobby Estalella, a September call-up from the minor leagues, twice took the Expos' ace deep and added a third home run in the ninth inning off Montreal reliever Anthony Telford as Philadelphia won 6-4. On September 10, Martinez scattered seven hits and struck out eight batters in a 5-4 win over the Pirates to improve his record to 17-7. With three starts remaining in the season, Pedro had a chance to win 20 games for the first time in his career. However, Pittsburgh ended those hopes with a 5-4 extra-inning win over the Expos September 15. Martinez struck out 10 in the no-decision, increasing his total to 284 in $226^{1}/3$ innings.

In his second-to-last start of the year, Martinez pitched his 13th complete game, struck out 12 Braves, and allowed just two earned runs. Unfortunately, the Expos' offensive problems continued. Altanta's Tom Glavine, the pitcher who had beaten Pedro just before the All-Star break, outdueled him again, allowing just one run as the Braves, the NL's winningest team, beat Montreal 2-1. It was Atlanta's ninth win in 10 games against the Expos. "With the stuff I had tonight, I could have beaten them," a dejected Martinez said after his seventh double-digit strikeout performance in his previous eight starts and his 18th of the season. Although the loss dropped his record to 17-8, he raised his strikeout total to 296.

Pedro was about to become the 14th pitcher to strike out 300 batters. In his final start of 1997, September 25 against the playoff-bound Florida Marlins, Martinez would need just four strikeouts to reach the plateau. Philadelphia's Schilling had already surpassed the mark, finishing with a league-leading 319 whiffs to set a new National League record for a right-handed pitcher.

Martinez came out strong. He struck out Florida batters in each of the first three innings, then hit the milestone by fanning Marlins shortstop Kurt Abbott for No. 300 in the fourth. Five more strikeouts would follow before Pedro left the game in the eighth, closing out the season with another masterful performance: four hits and just one earned run allowed. Once again, however, Montreal could not score with its ace on the mound and Pedro did not get credit for the decision, although the Expos scored twice in the ninth inning to win 3-2.

"I'm really proud to be with the guys [on the 300-strikeout list]," said Martinez after becoming just the third right-hander in NL history, and the first Latin American pitcher, to strike out 300. "There's a lot of Hall of Famers there. That means a lot to me."

"I was confident he'd get it. Whatever else he gets [like the Cy Young Award] I don't know," said Alou. "This is the best I've ever seen anybody pitch since I've been evaluating talent. He's been doing it with style all year. He has a 1.90 ERA. How many bad games did he have?"

Very few. Martinez finished the year leading the league in ERA, batting average allowed (.184) and complete games (13). He was second in strikeouts (305) and shutouts (4) and fourth in wins. Pedro also became the first pitcher to strike out 300 and finish with an ERA lower than 2.00 since Steve Carlton did it for the Phillies in 1972.

On November 11, members of the Baseball Writers' Association of America elected him the league's 1997 Cy Young Award–winner. He received 25 of 28 first-place votes and 134 points, easily outpacing runner-up Maddux, who finished with 75 points.

CHAPTER SEVEN
Baseball's Biggest Contract

Although he was thrilled to win the Cy Young Award, Pedro Martinez's future was up in the air after the final pitch he threw in the 1997 season. He knew it was very likely that the game against the Marlins would be his last appearance in a Montreal uniform.

The Expos' star pitcher had made over $3.5 million in 1997, but he was sure to receive an even bigger salary if he tested the free-agent market when he became eligible in 1998. After Expos general manager Jim Beattie said it was unlikely that his team would be able to sign him to a long-term deal, Martinez prepared to join the long list of Expos stars who were traded when their salaries got too high.

"I know I'm going to be traded. . . . I'm sad about it, not mad," Martinez told *USA Today*. "It's [the Expos'] politics, and that's the way they do things."

He was interested in playing for a contender and considered Florida. The Marlins had won the 1997 World Series, and Miami was just 90 minutes from the Dominican Republic. His interest was cooled when owner Wayne Huizenga began trading away the key members of his championship team, however. He was also interested in returning to the Dodgers; older brother Ramon was still a key member of their pitching staff, and younger brother Jesus was working his way through Los Angeles' minor-league system.

One week after the Cy Young Award announcement, another press conference was held involving Pedro Martinez. This time, the Expos announced that Martinez had been dealt to the Boston Red Sox for three minor-

league pitchers. The deal had been made while he was spending time with his family in the Dominican Republic.

Ironically, Boston's general manager, Dan Duquette, had been GM in Montreal during 1993 and arranged the trade of Delino DeShields for Martinez. The pitcher would also be reunited with his former pitching coach in Montreal, Joe Kerrigan, who had left the Expos for Boston after the 1996 season.

Pedro is all smiles at a news conference at Fenway Park in December 1997 where he formally announced that he had signed a six-year $75 million deal to pitch for the Red Sox. The deal made Martinez the highest paid player in baseball at that time.

Red Sox fans were understandably excited to add the best pitcher in baseball to their starting rotation. Unlike Montreal, Boston is a city that has a strong baseball following. Unfortunately, the history of the Red Sox is filled with frustration. The team's last World Series victory was in 1914; after the Series, they traded their best young pitcher—a fellow named George "Babe" Ruth—to the New York Yankees. Ruth went on to revolutionize baseball as a prodigious home-run hitter, and the Sox never recovered. Boston's failures—such as in 1978 when the Red Sox led the AL East by 13 games in July, then faltered during the last two months of the season, allowing the Yankees to finish in a tie for first, then win the division in a one-game playoff—are often attributed to the "Curse of the Bambino."

Perhaps the most frustrating moment in Boston's history came in Game Six of the 1986 World Series against the New York Mets. With a 3-2 series lead and two outs in the ninth inning, Boston's first baseman Bill Buckner let a routine ground ball dribble between his legs. That scored a run, and the Mets rallied to win the game and knot the Series. New York then took the seventh game to win the world championship.

Boston hoped to compete for the American League East title—and break its World Series jinx—in 1998; the addition of Martinez would solidify a shaky pitching staff. Duquette made some other moves to improve 1997's 78-84 Boston squad: he signed reliever Dennis Eckersley as a bullpen set-up man for closer Tom Gordon and traded for a pair of good defensive players in speedy outfielder Darren Lewis and slugging catcher Jim Leyritz.

Local sportswriters were thrilled by their team's new acquisitions, especially Martinez. Columnist Bob Ryan of the *Boston Globe* wrote, "With this move [the Red Sox] have announced to the world that ... they are tired of being out of pennant races by Memorial Day. They have had enough of the New York-Baltimore divisional tyranny. . . . They want to win now.

"It could be a wonderful year. . . . Pedro Martinez is one awesome pitcher."

Pedro (left front) appeared at the Carlos Baerga Celebrity Softball Game in San Juan, Puerto Rico on December 14, 1997. The game raised money for an AIDS pediatric cemter in Puerto Rico.

First, though, Boston had to sign Martinez to a long-term contract. Initial reports indicated that the pitcher did not want an extended deal with the Red Sox, but he downplayed those rumors. If he had been considering leaving Boston after the 1998 season, a visit to the city on December 11 may have changed those feelings. Several hundred Red Sox fans were waiting at the airport when his plane landed, and they cheered and chanted the pitcher's name.

"They were yelling and waving flags, and someone had a sign that said We Love You, Pedro," Martinez said. "That night I said to someone, 'I think I love Boston already.'" The next day, he signed a six-year, $75 million contract with the Red Sox. The contract was baseball's richest ever, topping Gary Sheffield's six-year, $61 million deal with the Florida Marlins, and Martinez's $12.5 million annual salary was higher than Greg Maddux's $11.5 million salary.

"We'd like to have a chance to win every year," Duquette explained to *Sports Illustrated*. "And the best way to do that and show our fans our intentions was with Martinez. He is a key piece to our having a good team. In a seven-game series, he could conceivably win three games, and there aren't many pitchers anywhere who can do that."

Duquette's comments made one thing clear: the young pitcher would be expected to help the Sox improve from six games under .500 in 1997 to a playoff spot—and a possible World Series berth—in 1998. Now the pressure would be on the young pitcher to prove that his great 1997 season was no fluke and justify his large contract.

CHAPTER EIGHT
Proving His Worth

In his first start of 1998, Martinez wasted no time in showing Red Sox fans why he was worth $75 million. In the team's opener April 1 at Oakland, he retired the first 11 American League batters that he faced. Martinez pitched seven strong innings, limiting the As to three hits and no runs while striking out 11 batters. The Sox won 2-0. "I felt pretty good. I'm happy with it. I hope every one is like this one," Martinez said after completing his first opening day start. "It's a great honor to be an opening day pitcher, but it's just one more game. I had all three pitches in command but used the breaking ball more."

But after winning their first two games of 1998, the Red Sox slumped, dropping two of three games to the Seattle Mariners and getting swept by the Anaheim Angels. In the opening game against Anaheim April 6, Martinez pitched a strong seven innings, striking out nine while allowing just seven hits and one run, but left with the game tied at 1-all. Reliever Tom Gordon gave up a run in the 11th inning that broke the deadlock, dropping the team's record to 3-5.

The Red Sox needed a dramatic comeback to win their season opener at Fenway Park. They were losing to Seattle 7-2 in the ninth inning until Mo Vaughn's grand slam capped a seven-run rally to give them the victory.

Boston seemed to be floundering. An inspiring pitching performance was needed, and Martinez was nothing short of magnificent the next night. In his first game at hitter-friendly Fenway Park, he dominated a Mariners' lineup featuring sluggers Ken Griffey Jr. and Alex

Rodriguez. Martinez allowed just two hits while striking out 12 in the complete-game, 5-0 shutout victory. He took command of the game early by retiring the first nine batters that he faced and finished strong by retiring the last 10 batters, five by strikeout. The victory marked the 29th time in his career that he had 10 or more Ks (strikeouts) in a game, and his strikeout of Rick Wilkins in the eighth inning was the 1,000th of his career. The Boston crowd chanted his name as his earned run average fell to a minuscule 0.39.

"The crowd reaction today was great for me. I just hope they know that I'm not going to be perfect all the time," Martinez said. "As long as they know that I'm going to go out every day like I did today and give 100 percent. That's all I need them to know. This is certainly a lot different and a lot better than Montreal."

The victory seemed to pull Boston together, and the team won its next five games, culminating in a 3-2, 10-inning victory over Cleveland. Although he didn't get credit for the win in that game, Martinez pitched very well, giving up four hits and two runs and striking out 12 without walking anyone. Boston lost the next night but rebounded to win its next seven games to improve to 17-6 on the season—good enough for first place in the American League East.

Even though the Red Sox continued to play well, they would not stay atop in league standings for long. The New York Yankees had started the season 1-4 but won 29 of their next 35 games to take command of the AL East standings.

The Detroit Tigers became the first AL team to solve Martinez. On April 22 he lasted just $5^1/3$ innings, giving up four runs and six hits to the Tigers, although Boston came back to win the game, 8-5.

Martinez seemed to be back to his old self in his next start, May 3, a pitching duel against Texas' Darren Oliver that Boston won, 2-1. Martinez improved to 3-0 on the season after the seven-inning, nine-strikeout performance in which he did not allow an earned run. On May 14 he pitched eight shutout innings against the Minnesota Twins, striking out 11 batters, but Boston lost the game, 2-1, in the 12th inning.

In his next start, despite not having his best stuff, Martinez picked up his fifth victory of the season in a 6-2 Red Sox win over the Chicago White Sox. The Boston fireballer struck out just five batters, but he allowed only four hits and one run in seven innings. "Pedro has had better games," Chicago manager Jerry Manuel commented afterward. "But tonight he showed why he's a great pitcher. He had a real good change-up that kept us off stride."

Over that four-game span, Martinez allowed just 4 runs in 29 innings for a 1.22 ERA, struck out 31 batters, and won three times.

On August 18, 1998, Pedro took over the league lead with his 18th victory.

His first loss came in his next outing, however, a 7-5 pasting by the Toronto Blue Jays. After allowing just three home runs during his first 10 starts of the season, Pedro gave up solo home runs to Jose Cruz, Jose Canseco, and Shawn Green. Earning the win for the Jays was 1996 AL Cy Young Award–winner Pat Hentgen, who won his fourth straight start, while the Boston ace gave up 12 hits, struck out eight, and walked one in $7^2/3$ innings. The disappointing outing marked the first time Martinez had allowed seven runs in a game in nearly four years.

Martinez's next outing did not get any better, as he allowed four runs and eight hits in just $5^1/3$ innings against the rival Yankees on May 31. However, he earned the win thanks to a 11-run third inning. Boston rode the offensive explosion to a 13-7 victory. Martinez was upset at being pulled from the game after giving up a three-run homer in the sixth inning.

His next start, on June 5, was also against a New York team, but this time it was an old National League foe. The Mets were the first team that the Red Sox would play in the second season of Major League Baseball's interleague play experiment, and they hammered Martinez for four home runs, beating the Sox 9-2. "Some days these things happen," Martinez said. "I'm struggling. It is not just this game. For the last three starts, I have not been doing my job. I'll just keep coming out and working hard."

"We all expect too much from Pedro," said Red Sox manager Jimmy Williams. "He's a human being. A night like this can happen. He's a great competitor, he's a fighter, and I know he'll fight back."

He got back into the win column in his next start, improving to 7-2 with a 10-6 victory over the National League–leading Atlanta Braves on June 10, but he was still unhappy with his pitching. For the second straight start, he gave up four home runs, lasting just 6²/3 innings. "Honestly, I wish I had the answer," a frustrated Martinez told reporters who asked about the 12 home runs he had given up over his previous four games and his 8.62 ERA during that period. "I made my pitches and I was strong. I threw the ball hard and was on top of every hitter. I'm a little bit embarrassed. That's not me. Things just didn't break the way I wanted.

"I don't think I can be any worse than this," he continued. "If I can [be worse], I ought to take off and go home. . . . I'm very concerned with my situation. I feel a little embarrassed to come out and [pitch] like that."

"He got a win, that's all we care about," said Williams, defending his star pitcher. "There were a lot of balls jumping out there tonight. His velocity was still good in the sixth and seventh. He was just mislocating with some breaking balls."

The good news was that as Martinez seemed to be coming apart, the rest of the Boston pitching staff was coming together.

Pedro was on the mound in 1998 in a game that clinched a playoff spot for the Red Sox.

Former Cy Young Award–winner Bret Saberhagen was second in the majors with eight wins, and Tim Wakefield, Steve Avery, and Derek Lowe had each been pitching well. In part, their success was due to the staff ace—a day after facing Martinez's 97-mph fastballs, teams had to adjust to Wakefield's slow-moving knuckleballs (clocked as low as 48 mph). But although the rest of the staff, a question mark at the start of the season, seemed to be rounding into shape, Boston fans knew their team's success or failure ultimately would depend on Martinez's getting out of his slump.

On June 16, Martinez pitched like he had put his troubles behind him, allowing just one run and striking out 11 in a 6-1 victory over the Chicago White Sox. The 11 Ks raised his season total to a league-leading 125, three ahead of Seattle fireballer Randy Johnson. "I felt strong, I felt healthy. I felt really comfortable about my stuff," Martinez said. In his next start five days later, he allowed just one hit and one run against the Tampa Bay Devil Rays to improve to 9-2. With a fastball clocked consistently at 97 mph, Martinez retired the first 11 batters he faced and the last 11 batters he faced, giving up the lone run on a walk and an RBI triple by Tampa's Miguel Cairo.

The win was Boston's ninth in 11 games, and the Red Sox improved to 40-27, 13 games over .500 for the first time since the end of the 1995 season. But despite their success—the Sox would have been leading any other division in the American League—they were still nine games behind the streaking Yankees (49-16), who had a chance to break major-league baseball's all-time record for victories in a season, 120.

Martinez proved he was back in top form in his next start, against the 1997 World Champion Florida Marlins. The right-hander shut down the Marlins, scattering five hits and a run over eight innings and striking out six as Boston won the interleague game 6-1. The game was especially notable for Pedro because it was played in Miami—and several hundred fans from the Dominican Republic showed up to wish him luck. "God, they drove me crazy," a smiling Martinez said of his enthusiastic supporters, including one woman who painted the Dominican flag on her cheek. "They were right on top of the bullpen, calling me, telling me to throw a shutout, telling me to strike out 20."

If the "backyard" win in Miami was a proud moment, Martinez's next game must have been a vindication. On July 2, Martinez faced the Expos for the first time in a Boston uniform. Montreal's starter was Carl Pavano—the rookie pitcher Montreal had received in the trade for Martinez. Boston's star pitcher dazzled his former teammates in a 15-0 rout. "Pedro didn't do anything that we haven't seen before," Montreal's F. P. Santangelo said. "All he did was go out there and shove it [in our faces]."

The victory was Martinez's 11th, tying him for the league lead with Yankee starters David Cone and David Wells and Rangers Rick Helling and Aaron Sele. He had not lost in over a month, since June 5. His strong first half of the season led to his third consecutive All-Star team selection. However, Mike Hargrove, manager of the American League's 1998 All-Star squad, decided to start Bartolo Colon, the star of his Cleveland Indians staff and, like Martinez, a native of the Dominican Republic. Martinez never appeared in the 1998 All-Star Game, which the American League won 13-8.

In his second start after the All-Star break, Martinez proved that he's still the best pitcher from the Dominican Republic—or nearly anywhere else, for that matter—

outdueling Colon 1-0 in a classic pitcher's duel. The nine-strikeout, four-hit performance was the first 1-0 complete game at Fenway in 11 years. Boston's lone run came on a solo home run by Midre Cummings.

Martinez was overpowering against the previous season's American League champions. After allowing two scratch singles in the second inning, he retired 15 Indians in a row before allowing another hit. "He had a great, great change-up," said Boston pitching coach Joe Kerrigan. "He threw 41 change-ups, 27 for strikes, and got 11 outs on his change-up. His fastball? He topped out at 97, was still throwing at 95 in the ninth, and sat at 94-95 all game. It was awesome. What a show for national TV [ESPN]. A baseball night, playoff atmosphere. It was good for the game."

"I knew this would be a low-scoring game and I knew I had to keep battling, because Colon is a very good pitcher," Martinez said after the July 15 game. "I know him from his days in the Dominican. He had excellent stuff tonight. . . . A game like this, you take it home and flavor [sic] it. Once I saw Midre hit that ball, I said, 'I will have to win with that one. I will win with that one.'"

In his next start six days later, also against the Indians, the Boston bats hammered out 10 runs and Martinez won his 13th game of the season. He allowed two earned runs in seven innings in the 10-7 victory. On July 26 he picked up his eighth win in nine decisions and improved to 14-3 with seven shutout innings against Toronto, avenging his loss to Hentgen earlier in the season.

In August, Martinez solidified his Cy Young credentials. He became the majors' second 15-game winner on August 1, pitching seven strong innings in an 11-3 win over the Angels. In a tough 4-3 loss to Texas a week later, he struck out 13 batters in $6^2/3$ innings. On August 19 he struck out 10 Rangers in a 4-1 win over Texas, and four days later came back to beat Minnesota, 5-1, to improve to 17-4.

On August 29 Martinez took over the league lead with his 18th victory, beating the Anaheim Angels 6-1. He struck out eight batters and allowed one run in eight innings, lowering his league-leading ERA to 2.67. "Pedro was nasty and abusive," said Angels shortstop Gary DiSarcina, who went 0 for 3 with two strikeouts. "He's probably the best pitcher I've seen since I'm in the big leagues. He made me feel like I was in the Little League."

With a month left in the season, Martinez seemed to be a sure bet to win the AL's Cy Young Award. But he fell into an inexplicable slump in the last month of the season. He lost his first three starts of September—the first time he had lost three consecutive games since 1995—allowing 11 earned runs in $28^1/3$ innings during that span.

Pedro's slump coincided with a Red Sox slide in the final month of the season. Leading the wild-card race by nine games at one point in August, Boston had faltered while the Toronto Blue Jays were the hottest team in baseball. The Jays cut the lead to three games at one point, but there wasn't enough time left in the season for them to catch the Red Sox.

Fittingly, Martinez was on the mound in the game that clinched a playoff berth, a 9-6 win, his 19th, over Baltimore in front of the home crowd at Fenway. It was not his best outing—he allowed five runs and six hits in $6^1/3$ innings with three walks and six strikeouts—but it was an important victory nonetheless. The win was Boston's 90th of the season, marking the team's best total since 1986.

Boston finished the season with a 92-70 record, 22 games behind the astonishing Yankees, who had set an American League record with 114 victories. Their first-round opponent would be the AL Central Division champion Cleveland Indians, who had come within one out of winning the 1997 World Series.

The Red Sox entered the playoffs with a record of recent postseason futility. The team had not won a playoff game since Game 5 of the 1986 World Series—going 0-13 since then. In their last playoff appearance, 1995, the Red Sox had been swept by the Cleveland Indians in three games. Pedro Martinez was Williams' choice to end that string in the first game of the 1998 postseason against the Indians.

Martinez responded with a good outing in his first postseason appearance. He pitched seven innings, allowing three runs and striking out eight as the Red Sox won easily, 11-3, at Cleveland's Jacobs Field to take a 1-0 lead in the best-of-five series. "Pedro had a good fastball and he was throwing his breaking stuff over," said Indians left fielder Brian Giles "I don't think he has to set you up. After being down 3-0, we felt we could find a way to win. But against Pedro, it's an uphill battle."

"It was great to know that you are ahead and have the advantage," said Martinez. "It was up to me to get the ball over and make the right pitches at the right time. We jumped out to a big lead, and I didn't want to walk anybody. I decided to go at them and if they hit the ball out, that was fine. I don't regret it."

But Cleveland had lost the first game of seven consecutive playoff series and come back to win four times. They showed they could come back one more time by winning the next two games, 9-5 and 4-3, to take a 2-1 series lead. One game away from playoff elimination, Williams and Kerrigan had a difficult decision to make: start the team's best pitcher on just three days' rest or use Pete Schourek, a late-season acquisition from Houston who had been a disappointing 1-3 with a 4.30 ERA with Boston during the stretch run.

Martinez practically begged the manager and pitching coach to let him pitch the pivotal fourth game. But Williams and Kerrigan decided to maintain their rotation by pitching Schourek, feeling Martinez would be more effective on four days' rest.

Most fans and the media were against the move, believing that Martinez was the team's best chance to remain alive in the playoffs for another game. As it turned out, Williams' decision turned out to be a good one, as Schourek put together a solid outing, allowing just two

Pedro is always willing to sign autographs for his fans. "It's part of my job," he says.

hits in five shutout innings and leaving the game with a 1-0 lead. But another Red Sox pitching decision—to remove reliever Derek Lowe, who held the Indians scoreless in the sixth and seventh, and bring in closer Tom Gordon an inning earlier than usual—back-

fired. Gordon, who usually pitched only in the ninth inning, had tied an American League record with 46 saves in 1998 and had successfully converted 43 consecutive save opportunities. But this time he tired, allowing two runs that gave the Indians the game, 2-1, and the series.

It was a disappointing end to what otherwise had been a very good Boston year. But Pedro could take some consolation in his excellent season—a career high in victories (19), the second-highest total of strikeouts in the AL (251), and a league-leading 2.89 ERA. And Red Sox fans could take consolation in the fact that Martinez will have worked hard over the winter to prepare for the 1999 season.

During the off-season, Monday through Saturday the Martinez brothers drive to the Olympic Training Center in Santo Domingo. There, they work out with a number of other professional baseball players from the Dominican Republic. A former Olympic trainer named Angel Presinol has a difficult conditioning program that is similar to the one used by great East German Olympic athletes in years past. The two-hour workouts include a four- to five-mile warmup run, followed by complex stretching, agility, strength, and aerobic exercises. After each session, Pedro and his brother go home to eat and rest. In the evenings, they spend another 90 minutes working out in Ramon's gym.

"Six days a week we work, one day we relax," Pedro said. "Stop working and you go right back to where you came from—nothing."

With an attitude like that, the Boston ace is sure to have many more successful seasons.

CHRONOLOGY

1971   Born October 25 to Paulino and Laopoldina Martinez in the Dominican Republic

1984   Brother Ramon is selected for Dominican Republic national team and signed to a professional baseball contract by Los Angeles Dodgers

1987   Dodgers offer Pedro a major-league contract

1988   Signs first major-league contract, with Los Angeles, on June 18; pitches for Santo Domingo rookie-league team and compiles 5-1 record; brother Ramon makes major-league debut with Dodgers

1990   Pitches with Great Falls rookie-league team

1991   Starts season at Single-A Bakersfield but does so well that Dodgers promote him to Double-A San Antonio and then to Triple-A Albuquerque, one step away from the major leagues

1992   Pitches at Albuquerque; named to Triple-A All-Star team; named one of 10 best prospects by *Baseball America*; makes major-league debut on September 24 against the Cincinnati Reds

1993   Called up to Dodgers after first week of the season; sets Los Angeles record for appearances by a rookie pitcher (65) and ends year with a 10-5 record and 2.61 ERA; traded to Montreal for second baseman Delino DeShields November 19

1994   Compiles 11-5 record and 3.42 ERA in first season as a starter with Expos; receives nickname Señor Plunk because of his tendency to pitch inside

1996   Wins 13 games and sets career highs in strikeouts, innings pitched, and complete games ; named to NL All-Star team for the first time; suspended for final game of 1996 and first seven games of 1997 after charging mound against Philadelphia Phillies

1997   Dominates National League hitters, allowing just a .184 batting average and striking out over 300 batters; named to NL All-Star team; wins NL Cy Young Award; traded to Boston November 18; signs richest contract in baseball history, a six-year, $75 million pact, December 12

1998   Named to AL All-Star team; wins career-high 19 games, helping Boston Red Sox reach the playoffs for the first time since 1995; wins first playoff appearance, 11-3, over Cleveland Indians

MAJOR LEAGUE STATS

YEAR	TEAM	ERA	W	L	Sv	G	IP	H	R	ER	BB	K	AVG A
1992	LA	2.25	0	1	0	2	8.0	6	2	2	1	8	.200
1993	LA	2.61	10	5	2	65	107.0	76	34	31	57	119	.201
1994	Mon	3.42	11	5	1	24	144.2	115	58	55	45	142	.220
1995	Mon	3.51	14	10	0	30	194.2	158	79	76	66	174	.227
1996	Mon	3.70	13	10	0	33	216.2	189	100	89	70	222	.232
1997	Mon	1.90	17	8	0	31	241.1	158	65	51	67	305	.184
1998	Bos	2.89	19	7	0	33	233.2	188	82	75	67	251	.217
Totals		2.98	84	46	3	218	1146	890	420	379	373	1221	.213

INDEX